Translated by Polly Lawson
First published in Dutch under the title *Het Geschenk voor het Kind* by Christofoor Publishers
First published in English in 2001 by Floris Books
© 1999 Cornelis Wilkeshuis, Jeska Verstegen, Christofoor Publishers
English version © 2001 Floris Books
British Library CIP Data available
ISBN 0-86315-349-6   Printed in Belgium

The Gift
for the Child

A Story by Cornelis Wilkeshuis

Illustrated by Jeska Verstegen

Floris Books

Far, far from here in the distant East, good King Balthasar lived in a huge palace with tall towers. Every evening he would climb up to the very tallest tower and for hours he would watch the stars.

In an old book of wisdom, the king had read that the stars were like shining letters written upon the night sky. If you could only read the letters, you would know the future.

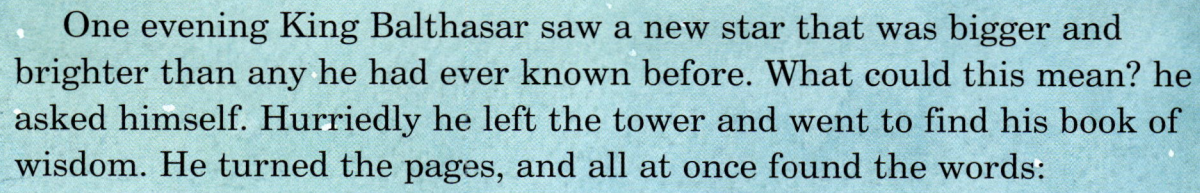

One evening King Balthasar saw a new star that was bigger and brighter than any he had ever known before. What could this mean? he asked himself. Hurriedly he left the tower and went to find his book of wisdom. He turned the pages, and all at once found the words:

A star shall appear in the heavens, shining more brightly than any other. This is a sign that a King is born, who will bring peace to all men.

"I shall go to greet the new King," Balthasar said to himself, "for I love peace better than war. Perhaps the young King will need my help."

Then Balthasar told his servants to saddle the camels and to get everything ready for a long journey.

"May we know where we are going?" asked the king's servants.

"I do not know," said Balthasar. "We shall simply follow the new star wherever it leads us."

The camels were soon saddled and the king and his followers made ready to set off on their strange journey.

Hearing all the hustle and bustle in the palace, the king's son woke and ran down to the courtyard to find out what was happening. In his arms he carried Pluto, the little white dog that went everywhere with him.

"Where are you going, father?" he asked.

"A new king has been born," said Balthasar. "Look, in the night sky there shines a new star. It is written that the new king will bring peace to mankind. I am going to follow the star and travel to greet the new-born Prince of Peace," he went on, "and I shall give him this golden cup."

"Please may I come too, father?"

"No, my child," was the answer. Then the camel-drivers blew on their flutes and the caravan departed.

The little prince went upstairs. He did not go back to bed but quickly got dressed. I want to go and see the new-born king too, he thought. I have not got such a fine cup as my father has, but I shall give him my best toys.

First he took the ball which a friend had just given him.
Then he chose his favourite book full of pictures of animals
and flowers. Then he called Pluto and told him about their
adventure.

With Pluto on the lead the little prince crept out of the palace. No one saw him leave. He crept past the gatekeeper who was fast asleep. Fortunately the dark night was already giving way to dawn. But the star still shone as brightly as before, showing the way.

The little prince and Pluto walked for miles and miles. They came to a wood at the edge of a village, and stopped to rest under a tree. To their surprise they heard a little girl crying in the wood.

"Why are you crying?" asked the little prince.

"Because no one will play with me," she sobbed.

"Why won't anyone play with you?" the little prince asked.

"They all laugh at me because of my torn dress and then they run away," answered the girl.

"Take this ball and then you will have a friend to play with," said the little prince kindly.

All day and all evening the little prince and Pluto
continued on their journey, following the star that shone
above the horizon. They both kept their eye on the star so that they
should not lose their way.

Soon the road took them to a wide river where they saw a huge hippopotamus with a bird on its back.

After a while, they came upon a little house. In the doorway an old man was leaning on a stick, looking very unhappy.

"What is the matter?" asked the little prince.

"My legs are hurting," complained the man, "and I cannot walk any more, and so I see nothing of the world as I once did."

"I know what you need," said the little prince. "I'll give you this beautiful book, full of pictures of flowers and animals, and you will have it always by you."

And together they looked at the book.

"There are also poems in it," cried the old man, surprised. "Thank you, now I can enjoy the beauty of the world again."

The days passed and the travellers became weary. The little prince had blisters on his feet and Pluto was limping. Both were beginning to miss the comfort of their own beds.

For a distance, they travelled along the great river in a boat,
still following the star which they watched day and night.

On land again, they came to a farm where they stopped to ask for food and shelter. In the house, there lived a boy of the same age as the little prince. The boy had been lying in bed for months with a crippling illness. He became envious when he saw how strong and healthy the little prince was. He did not want to talk to him and hid his face in the pillow.

But the little prince called Pluto and the dog sprang straight away up on to the sick boy's bed. He licked and tickled him until the boy turned round laughing.

The little prince knew what he had to do. He pressed Pluto's lead into the sick boy's hand and quietly left the boy playing happily and stroking the dog.

Once the little prince was outside he felt tears come into his eyes. He had given everything away, even Pluto his best friend. But when he thought of the poor girl and the old man and heard the sick boy laugh, he wiped the tears away. He walked on as far as he could until he became too tired to go further. There in the bushes, he lay down and fell into a deep sleep.

The little prince woke up when it was dark. He looked around puzzled. Had he been asleep all day? Feeling refreshed, he went happily on his way. The animals in the wood watched him go by as if to wish him well. But the little prince kept his eyes fixed only on the star. All at once the star stopped quite still.

The little prince looked and saw a rough
stable. Could the new King be born here?

He walked up and very carefully opened the door. Inside he
saw a man and a woman and a baby lying in a simple cradle. Was
this the new-born King, the Prince of Peace?

Then he saw his father and, beside him, two other kings.
The three kings laid their gifts at the child's feet: a vase of
costly myrrh, a silver bowl with frankincense and Balthasar's
cup of gold.

The little prince went to greet the child, but he hardly dared look up. He was ashamed that he had nothing left to give ...

But the mother understood. She pressed the little prince warmly to her and whispered: "The child is very happy that you have nothing left to offer. The joy you gave to others is the most beautiful gift you could have brought him."